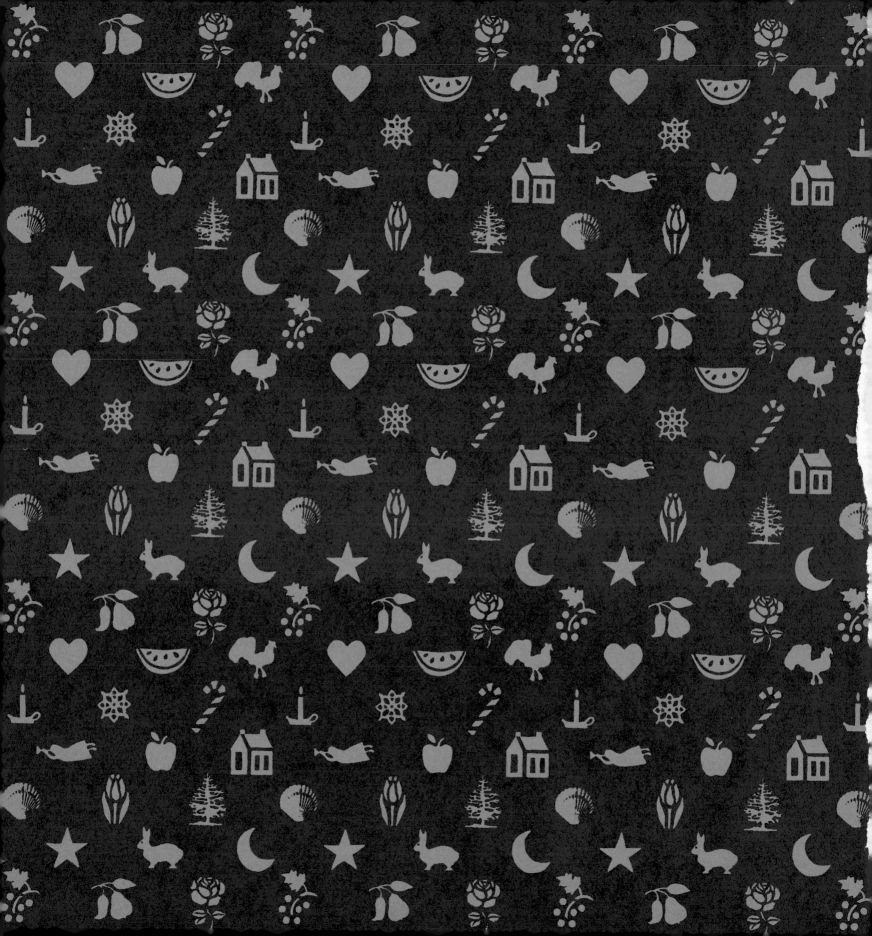

LIVING HOME

FIXING UP
AND ENTERTAINING
WITH
AMERICAN COLORS,
PATTERNS AND FORMS.

BY RAYMOND WAITES
BETTYE MARTIN
AND NORMA SKURKA

DESIGN BY RAYMOND WAITES
DESIGN ASSOCIATE: JANICE WARNER

1817

HARPER & ROW, PUBLISHERS, New York
Cambridge, Philadelphia, San Francisco, London, Mexico City, São Paulo, Sydney

THE AMERICAN DREAM

Michael Skott

Colonial Welcome

Affluent Americans wanted to live the way their British forebears did. This American counterpart to English Georgian manor houses was built in 1815 and still stands on Main Street in Haverhill, New Hampshire. The blue door is adorned with a wildflower garland that you can make (see page 60).

TO
WILLIAM MUSHAM:
WITHOUT BILL
ALL THIS
WOULD NOT BE
POSSIBLE

Ripe for Preservation

Truly American, this house is a mixture of whimsy and function. Although sadly neglected, it is salvageable. The straight roofline indicates that the rafters and roof are still strong. Stranded by the side of a highway, this house is probably doomed. But look at the loss: a relic of the farm life that reared generations of Americans.

PORCH SALE

eter Neumann

AMERICA'S VISUAL VOCABULARY

A FOCUS ON THE COLORS, PATTERNS, FORMS THAT SURROUND US

This is a totally different kind of design book. In it, we show the origins of American design and the fundamental elements from which it grew. But more importantly, we focus on the colors, patterns and forms that are all around us. Since early childhood, each of us has built-in images, impressions and memories of the towns and countryside that reared us. Those impressions are a part of us—whether we know it or not. We may have taken those images for granted, but they form America's visual vocabulary. One needn't travel far from the cities to encounter the artifacts of our heritage: a barn in the midwest emblazoned with hearts; houses smiling with gingerbread confections in rainbow colors; window shutters with cutouts of arrows and moons; white clapboard churches dominating the village green; and all across the country, barns of red, yellow and green with towering silos.

Instinctively, we are products of this imagery. Deep in our psyche, we love America's exuberant spirit. We respond to it intuitively because it is a part of every American. As we travel abroad, we may love the chateaux and palaces of Europe. But they are not ours. When we come home, we are glad to leave behind those aristocratic pretensions. We Americans are basic and independent.

America's forefathers and mothers celebrated the simple objects of their everyday existence. The most loved and appreciated of these objects, today considered folk art, are those which were made by hand and stamped indelibly with their maker's imprint. Our ancestors turned the simple house shape into the classic schoolhouse quilt. Farm animals became themes for weathervanes, house pets were worked into motifs for hooked rugs. We continue to marvel at the way discards were turned into art—fabric scraps into patchwork quilts and rag rugs, iron scraps into signs and weathervanes, natural materials such as willow, splint and rush into baskets and chair seats, twigs into furniture. We Americans are "do-ers." This book will provide the tools to create unique living environments.

Earlier generations reveled in being alive in a new land. The farm influence is a recurring motif in American folk art. To this day, traveling from the potato fields of Long Island to the truck farms of California, one is struck by the vast acreage still under cultivation. Despite the incursion of heavy industry and housing developments, America is still largely a nation of farm folk.

Nature provided a powerful model for native crafts and colors. America's geographical variety and richness shaped an attitude and a regional architecture. We can see this in the Southwest, where adobe was as natural to native builders as was wood in the heavily forested East. The architecture of the Gulf States and California reflects climatic conditions: stilt houses in swampy Louisiana, open, rambling homes in sun-drenched Florida and southern California. The awesome mountains, the quiet plains of wheat and corn, forestlands so dense that light flickers through in kaleidoscopic patches, oceans of desert sand—in each area builders accommodated themselves to the land, and the land, in turn, offered its color and images to the imaginations of its inhabitants.

So much has contributed to our national character. No single culture can be said to have formed this pioneering nation. The heritage of the English along the Eastern seaboard has to be balanced against the Spanish colonization on the opposite coast. And while the French, Dutch, and Spanish were carving out enclaves on the nation's shores, an ancient Indian civilization was flourishing in the interior. In the arid Southwest, their building techniques are still used in the adobe construction of New Mexico and Arizona. America continued to take in pioneers and our new immigrants from every land enrich our culture with their own ethnic heritage.

From this marvelous polyglot of sources has emerged an American visual vocabulary. It is unique. It is as much a manifestation of the imported dreams and ideals of our ancestors as it is a result of geographical expediency. Adapting, refining, modifying, evolving—that is the essence of the American identity. The myriad traditions brought to these shores are given a *new* spirit; they are adapted and reshaped to become truly American.

By the middle of the last century another factor entered: technology. Railroads linked the urban centers with rural towns; electricity reached out to the farthest outposts by the Rural Electrification program of 1935; automobiles brought freedom of movement; the airplane gave instant access to any part of the world; television opened up ideas and social interchange on a global scale. Finally, and most significantly, space science planted a man on the moon and changed for all time our planetary conceit. Our earth, viewed from the moon, appeared exceedingly fragile and vulnerable. These technological advances changed our view of the world—they brought us closer to each other and to other cultures—and our designs changed too.

In the light of 20th-century developments, the values that built America seem all the more precious. The accomplishments of the past two hundred years are not simply nostalgic reminiscences. Country things that our great-grandparents made, hooked rugs, country cupboards, twig furniture, stoneware, needlework, and quilts are part of America's visual vocabulary. What we sense in these humble objects is a spirit that is America. It is a spirit that fashions beauty and charm out of necessity.

Collecting and living with these fragments of American design brings an awareness of our roots into daily life. Adapting colors from nature's palette results in beautifully livable color schemes for the interior and exterior of our homes. Surrounding ourselves with natural things, such as exposed wood beams, pine furniture, fresh flowers, softens the hard edges of our hectic lives. Objects from the past provide the springboard for many of the fabrics, patterns, bed linens, dishes and other furnishings found on the market today. And yet schemes that build on the old designs have a fresh, contemporary flavor. Old and new mix harmoniously in the most modern living homes.

This, then, is the message of this book: Look around you. See the colors, patterns and shapes of our tradition in a new light. Learn from what you see. Use that knowledge to enrich and enliven your daily life.

HOW TO DESIGN YOUR ROOMS

There isn't a book we know that tells you, in terms you can understand, how to create a room you'll love. Ours does. Here is concrete advice. Our suggestions are not ironclad rules. We do not believe in rules. These suggestions are simple tools to help you decide what you like, how to use color, and how to use what you love in your home. Working in the way we outline here may not be everyone's solution to designing rooms. Try it, if you can; our method works.

DESIGN BY COLOR

1 Color is the foundation of this book. It is also the basis around which to design your rooms. Color unifies everything in a room, and it makes decorating decisions easier. You will make fewer mistakes. Here's how to do it.

DISCOVER WHAT YOU LOVE

2 What are the colors that you like? Is it the white of old ironstone, the glow of silver, the red of a patchwork quilt? Is it the blue of export china or old spatterware? Take out the things you own and love. Group them together by color on a tabletop. Notice how color gives a coherence

to different shapes, textures, periods, and scale. Study the grouping. Does it appeal to you? If so, what other things work with the collection?

CLIP MAGAZINES

3 Magazines are great sources of ideas. When you see something appealing—an armoire, a fabric, a window treatment—clip it out. Paste the picture in a notebook for your working design portfolio. This becomes your "hope chest" of dreams. Lay these pages alongside the other things you've selected. Do they complement each other in style and mood?

DEVELOP A MOOD

4 Your furnishings and fabrics create the room's mood. Silks and brocades will result in a formal room. Cottons, chintzes, homespun fabrics result in a more relaxed, comfortable one. Think about this as you develop the room's mood. Work heirlooms and other sentimental objects into the plan. Give family photographs, an old rocker, anything with special meaning, a place in your design. These elements make your room unique. If you love country themes and you are an electronics addict, store your equipment in an armoire. Or leave it out amidst the country things, since we do live in the 20th century! Live with the past today. Well designed objects from different times work well together.

BE CONFIDENT

5 Follow your taste. Don't let your family and friends talk you out of your ideas. Throughout this book are examples of odd and eccentric things loved by their owners—an amusing ceramic cabbage collection, a stenciled hearth. These objects make wonderfully personal rooms.

DON'T TRY FOR PERFECTION

6 Perfect rooms are intimidating. People don't feel comfortable in them. They look fine in a magazine, but we miss the personal touches that make them real. If a vase has a chip in it or the table is scratched, don't discard it. The baby or the puppy will only add other chips and scratches anyway. Be relaxed about the furnishings in your rooms. Imperfections are often the ingredients of a room's unique style. Own objects that you feel comfortable about using. Too many fineries stay locked in the cupboard until guests arrive. Use what you have and love. That's what a living home is all about.

TEST THE DESIGN

7 Once you've decided on the color, test it on the wall. Paint or wallpaper a section in the color or pattern. Put the table with your objects on it next to the wall. Add a place setting. Now live with this for a few days. You'll see if you tire of it. If not, you are ready for a firm commitment and investment.

DRESS THE ROOM

8 Be on the lookout for the unusual—those unexpected finds at an antique fair or flea market. A pitcher is great for serving wine; a child's wood wagon may become a magazine rack. There's no perfect place for any object. Move your belongings around. Try them in different rooms and different places. Rooms have a life of their own.

MAKE A LIVING HOME

9 We cannot duplicate the past. We can only learn from it. We visit museum rooms and historic houses for ideas, but we don't want to live in them. Mix the historic with the modern. We are a nation with relaxed attitudes about living. Make yours a living home.

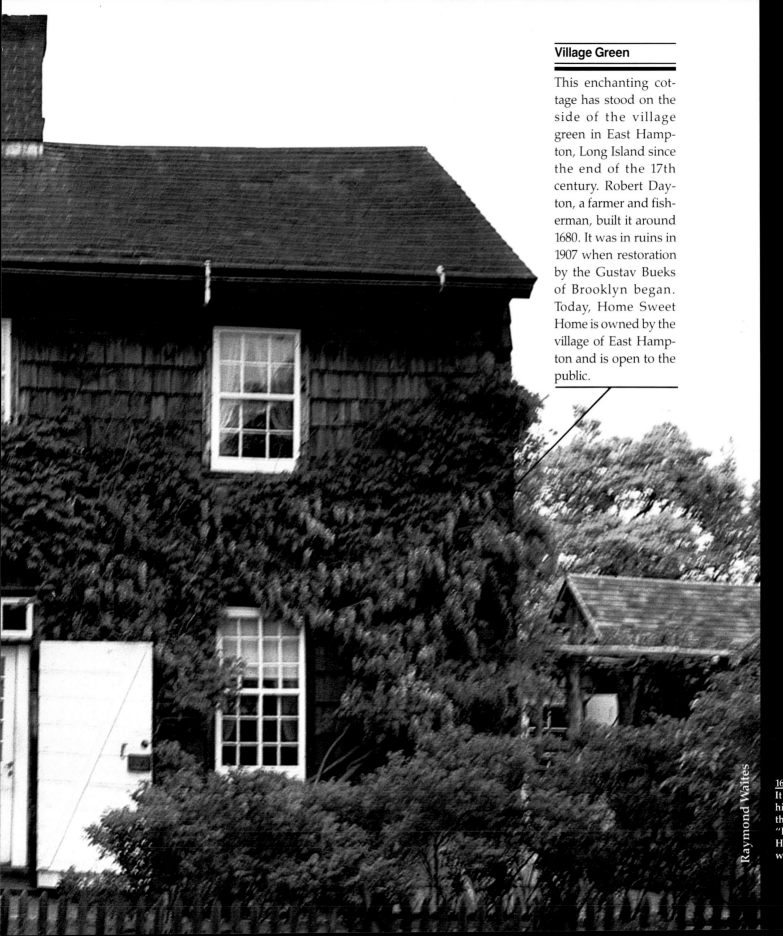

Village Green

This enchanting cottage has stood on the side of the village green in East Hampton, Long Island since the end of the 17th century. Robert Dayton, a farmer and fisherman, built it around 1680. It was in ruins in 1907 when restoration by the Gustav Bueks of Brooklyn began. Today, Home Sweet Home is owned by the village of East Hampton and is open to the public.

Raymond Waites

1680's SALTBOX
It was about this historic house that the song "Home Sweet Home" was written.

CLASSIC CAPE

East Coast Traditional

America's Eastern Seaboard is replete with cottages and small Cape-style houses covered with hand-hewn shingles that were allowed to weather naturally to a rich, silvery gray. Window and door trims were invariably painted white, providing a pleasing contrast to the weathered wood. Today, architects are returning to the traditional shingles and white trim and rediscovering the simple, elegant shapes of early Colonial architecture.

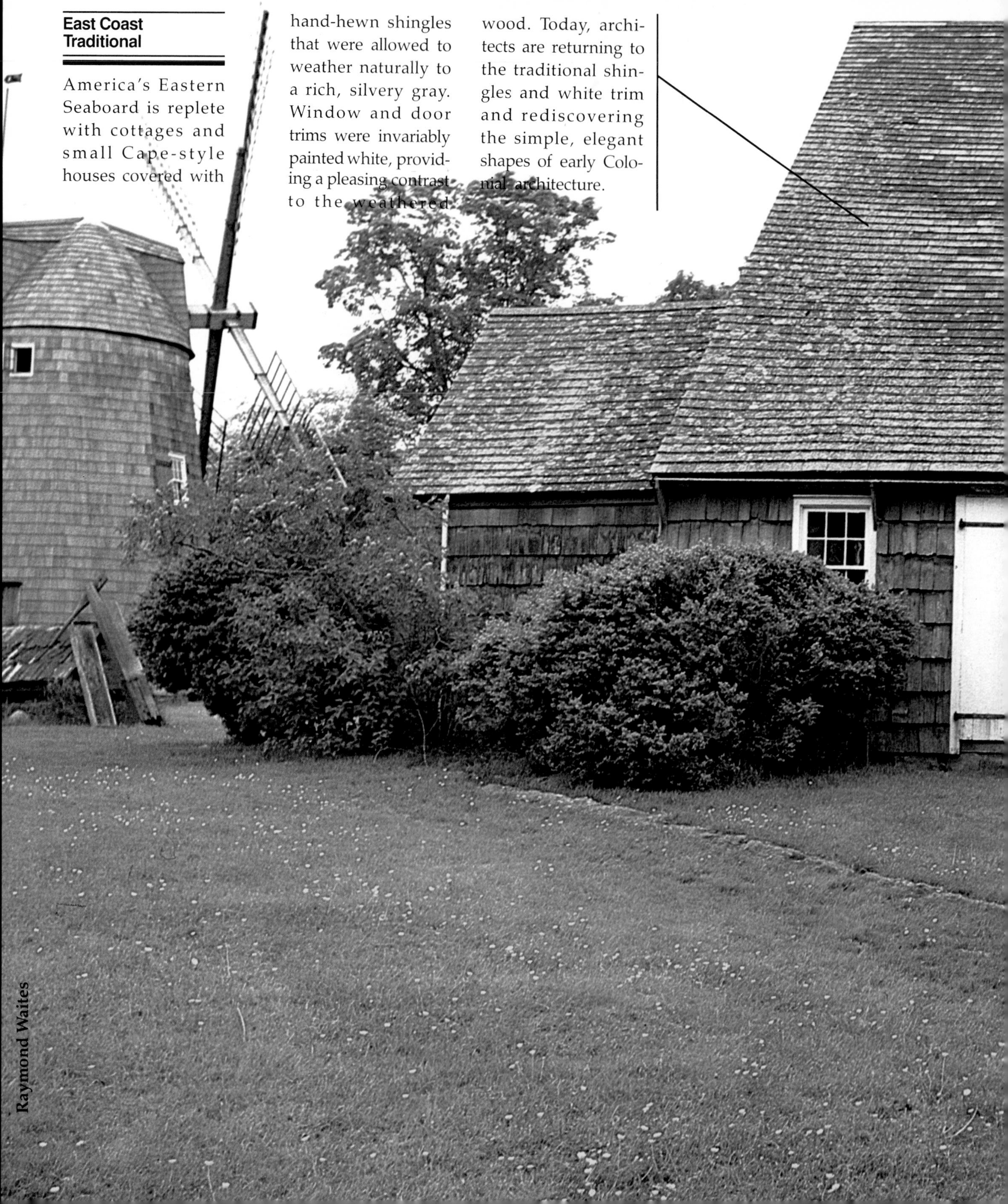

USE AND NDMILL
broad roof his 17th-cen- cedar shake age slopes vn to the t-floor win- vs. House windmill in East mpton, Long nd, where of the larg- concentra- ns of wind- ls can be nd.

Raymond Waites

Multiple Use

Barns served as stable, feed and grain bin, storage space, and garage. The exceptionally tall doors allowed a horse-drawn cart to travel through the barn without the rider having to dismount.

Colonial High-Tech

Barns are the work-horses of indigenous American architecture and are so easily converted into modern homes, like the one on page 118.

Raymond Waites

CEDAR SHAKE BARN

OUTBUILD
Barns are th
workhorses
indigenous
American
architecture

Lilo Raymond

CLAPBOARD CHURCH

Quaker Notes

Members of the Society of Friends were called Quakers because George Fox, the Englishman who founded the sect in 1650, bade them to "tremble at the word of the Lord." They have no ordained clergy and no liturgy, and their meetinghouses are made as simple as possible. In the life of these early colonists, the public meetinghouse was the social center.

Friends Meetinghouse

The harsh, disciplined life of the settlers is clearly expressed in the austerity of this exquisite meeting-house built in 1787 in Vermont. Its simple peaked roof, repeated in miniature in the side extension, the regularity of the windows, and the unadorned facade give the building an awesome power and spirituality. This is one of the finest examples of Colonial architecture.

BAYOU COLONIAL

Barry O'Rourke/Stock Market

BAYOU COUNTRY COLONIAL
Heat and humidity as well as French settlers shaped plantation houses of the Deep South.

Built to Stay Cool

This plantation house, a Cajun farmhouse in Louisiana, is a pavilion with the living area on the second story, the kitchen and utility area below. The bonnet roof shades the "galerie" or verandah. By raising the second story on stilts, cool air is allowed to circulate.

Masonry Tradition

Stone buildings are rare in America, a nation of wooden architecture. But pockets of a masonry tradition do exist, especially where the Germans and Dutch settled. This tradition combined with local stone to produce one of America's best-loved houses—the farmhouses of Pennsylvania, New Jersey, and New York.

Raymond Waites

FIELDSTONE
This stone barn is part of Greenfield Village, an historic museum, open to the public, near Detroit.

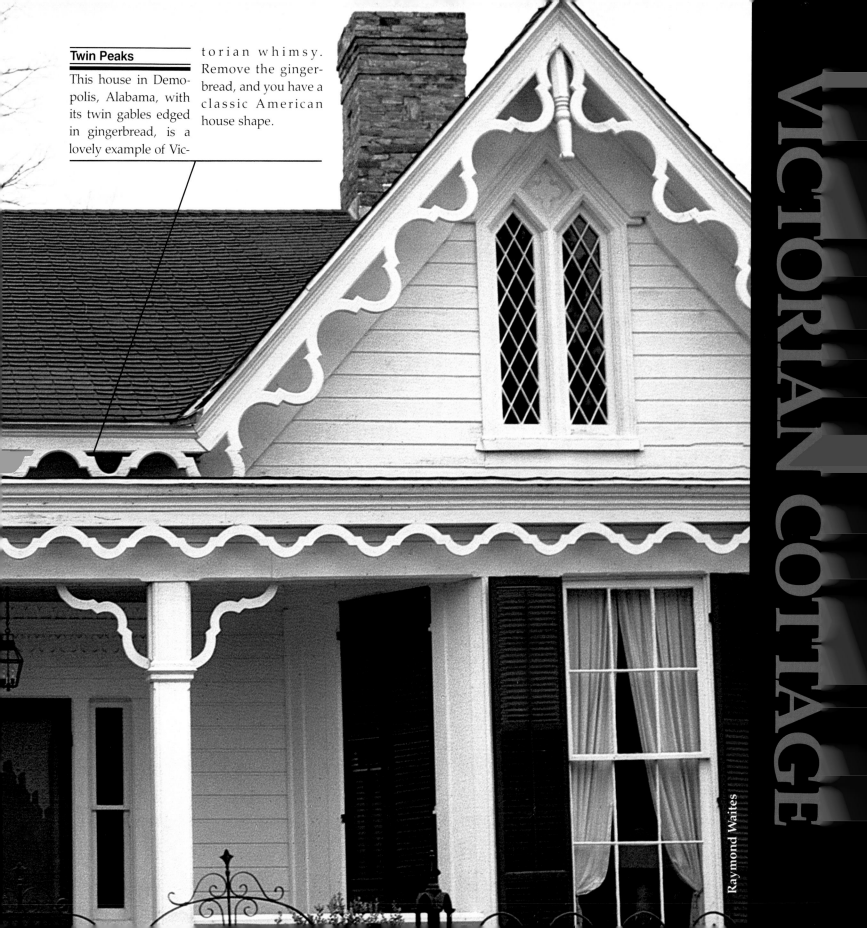

Twin Peaks

This house in Demopolis, Alabama, with its twin gables edged in gingerbread, is a lovely example of Victorian whimsy. Remove the gingerbread, and you have a classic American house shape.

Raymond Waites

Doors are silent pronouncements. They tell us both about the style and architecture of a building and about the people who live there. Doors were always subject to shifts in taste and fashion, much more so than windows or even the house shape: When a new style of architecture came along, it was

Everybody's Doorway

Overhead and side lights, and the curtain behind the large central window of this doorway convey a friendly spirit.

first manifested in the front door.

The front door of a house is usually meant to impress, and the builders of stately homes lavish attention on it. It proclaims the importance of the house, and thus, of the family who lives there. Through the ages, front doors have been adorned with details of classical architecture; they have been flanked by columns, pillars, and pilasters, inset

Light Entry

Early houses of the Eastern Seaboard would often have "lights" or windows above the door in order to bring light into the hallway.

JOHN EARLE

LILO RAYMOND

Mystery Cove

Hewn into the side of a cliff, a magical opening seems to lead deep into the earth. This is one of the earliest forms of housing in America; the cliff dwellings of the Pueblo Indians.

with windows, topped by pediments, friezes, and dentils.

There are, of course, different kinds of doors to suit different purposes. So, impressive as the front door might be, others are designed to be unobtrusive or almost invisible. Back doors, for example, are usually plain and ordinary. They greet us like old friends, lead us into familiar territory.

Blue Moons

Shutters, painted a bright blue, have amusing cutouts shaped like moons. Such playful touches are found on many American houses.

RAYMOND WAITES

LILO RAYMOND

Doorways also exhibit strong regional and ethnic differences. Those in New England look completely different from their counterparts in New Orleans or in the Far West. These differences reflect more than the varying styles that characterize each region. They express the aspirations of those who settled in that part of the country and who brought the tastes of their native lands across the ocean. Such regional variations in doorways lend vitality to the street scene. They make walking tours in a strange city so full of surprise.

The closed door gives a clue to who and what resides within; it is the outer limit of someone else's private world. Beyond the closed door is a special world—to enter is to venture into another's territory. A closed door to a

Windmill Door

This doorway to a windmill on the eastern shore of Long Island has been weathered by the salt air. The door is made of a row of planks held together on the inside with wood braces.

Log Cabin

The flapping of the screen door against the frame was a familiar sound to scores of Americans who fled to country cottages in summer.

RAYMOND WAITES

MICHAEL SKOTT

place we've never been signals excitement. There is a sense of expectation, like being handed a wrapped present. What's inside? Often, the first glimpse into a new space is the occasion for a silent thrill. But first one must traverse that portal to a place that is new and unknown. That's the reason why we are drawn to those doors that give a sense of welcome, either by color, hardware, or with a wreath or garland.

Wood and Stucco

Compare this blocky, rustic door in New Mexico to the doorway pictured beside it to see how far the decoration of the American door has come.

Full of Fancy

At the turn of the century, it was considered ideal to live in a fanciful cottage with a trellis, lattices, and lacy gingerbread trim. Here even the doorframe is curved.

RAYMOND WAITES

RAYMOND WAITES

31

Smooth versus rough; glass transom versus tightly closed shutters—these are the contrasts that keep the eye interested in this Santa Fe doorway.

Doors offer a wealth of visual pleasure. And beauty doesn't occur only in the formal doorway; nor is it exclusively the builder's art. House owners frequently add individual touches to those of the architect or builder. A bright red door, or a doorway wrapped by a garland of flowers, or a door marked by a

The importance of this staunch dwelling and its inhabitants is announced by the Federal doorway and stairway. It adorns a Nantucket residence.

RAYMOND WAITES

BARRY O'ROURKE/STOCK MARKET

32

beautiful wreath all give different messages about the inhabitants.

And nature herself can work magic on a door, weathering the wood to a soft and welcoming texture and color. So even the most rustic of doorways can exert a powerful charm. Many wonderful old doors were made from a single plank of solid wood or several extra-wide ones grooved together. Dec-

Weatherworn

Weather lends a patina to all things. In this rustic farmhouse dwelling, weather has gnarled the paneled door and siding to textural richness.

ades of weather and wear etched them with a rich, natural patina. Yet, it is often the whim of a new owner of an old house to replace such doors. This is a mistake since these aged doors are frequently the most beautiful of all.

Because doorways are so visible and yet so personal, make yours a welcoming sight to those you know as well as to strangers passing by.

Fine Restoration

Shadows emphasize the deep reveals and outline of this Italianate doorway in Providence, Rhode Island.

MICHAEL SKOTT

BARRY O'ROURKE/STOCK MARKET

Windows might be called the "eyes" of the house. Through them, the house views the world and its surroundings just as we catch glimpses into the house's inner realm. Over the years, the role and function of windows has changed dramatically. Early settlers were more concerned with conserving heat and protecting themselves from the elements than they were with admiring the view. For centuries there were no windows as we know them today. Glass was not readily available and it was expensive. It was manufactured in this country only rarely until 1739, when Caspar Wistar established the first large scale and successful glasshouse. Until then, oiled

Vine Covered

The owners of this shingled cottage on Long Island can open their classic 12-over-12 window to allow the sweet smell of the ancient wisteria to waft into their house.

Shutters as Accent

Shutters, painted an unconventional bright red, add a cheery note to a small Cape Cod house with tongue-and-groove siding.

RAYMOND WAITES

ROY SCHNEIDER/STOCK MARKET

paper or fabric was a common means of covering the window. Early windows, or "wind holes," were small openings which let in a little air and light, with a shutter like device to close it up again. Because security was also a factor in this country's early years, small windows and tightly drawn shutters with small light slits secured the house from outside attacks.

Industrial Window

A familiar sight in the older sections of cities are the arched windows of warehouses (fast being converted into living lofts) with their tight-fitting shutters.

As America prospered, windows grew in style and importance. Each architectural period found its expression in unique window forms. In Colonial times windows were rather evenly spaced across the front and sides of the house. Because of its scarcity and the difficulty of transporting or manufacturing large

Victorian Oculus

An ornamental window lights the entrance hall of a late 1800s house in the Midwest. The white trim is pleasing against the blue siding.

sheets of glass, individual panes were small: the older the house the smaller (and consequently the more numerous) the panes. In England, houses were taxed if their windows exceeded a certain number and this practice was probably enforced in some of the British colonies.

By Federal times windows grew larger. Twelve-over-twelve paned windows replaced six-over-eight double-sash windows. By Victorian times windows evolved into the four-paned, double-sash windows that are found throughout the country, particularly in the Midwest.

The grander the house, of course, the grander the windows. They are clues to how prosperous or how aspiring were the houses' builders.

Gingerbread Window

Ornamental grillwork became increasingly popular as the 18th century waned. Here is a choice example of the exuberance it lends to a porch or veranda.

American Simplicity

The simplest windows evoke a spirit that is uniquely American. The geometry of the white frame, lintels and sashes, plays against the narrow white clapboards.

RAYMOND WAITES

LILO RAYMOND

All architectural periods exhibit great interest and variety in window design. Some of the most beautiful windows date from the late 18th through the 19th century. We have only to visualize the elaborate, lighted doorways of the Georgian mansion, where the side lights and over-window are outlined in delicate tracery

Animating Mullions

Church windows delight because of the few controlled touches that enliven the overall austerity. In this case, the livening touch is provided by the unusual mullions of the top tier.

to feel a sense of elegance and luxury. The Palladian window, a design imported from Italy via England, is a three-part window capped by a semilune over the center. Used extensively through late Colonial and Federal times, it's still one of the most elegant of all window designs.

Sometimes windows have characterized whole cities, stamping them

Tall and Narrow

Shutters accentuate the narrowness of a doorway in New Orleans. The straight-edged lintel crowns the arch of the shutters.

LILO RAYMOND

RAYMOND WAITES

37

with a unique architectural identity. San Francisco comes to mind. The ubiquitous three part bay window animates the street scene for blocks on end. (Was the bay window so called because it overlooked San Francisco Bay?) The uniform rows of Victorian houses with their projecting bay windows play no small part in that city's reputation for stealing our hearts. Or, think about Nantucket or Cape Cod and you have an immediate image of repetitious windows.

White Wood

Gingerbread trim turns paired windows into a lighthearted valentine.

Adobe

Greek Revival even reached the Southwest. Here is a covered porch with a classical dentil frieze.

Specialized windows through various periods were functional as well as decorative. The charming eyebrow windows, a row of shallow windows located just below the roof line of the story-and-a-half Federal farmhouse, is an example. Attic windows set in the hip roofs also took many delightful forms. The oculus and bull's eye windows, round or oval as the names suggest, were frequently used in the houses' gable ends.

Red Brick

Red might almost be called America's national color. In brick, it characterizes houses, warehouses, and even whole cities.

Classic Contrast

Window trim adds a decorative accent to a clapboard house.

Lighthearted

A romantic farmer proclaimed his love of life from the roof of a Midwestern barn.

Pastel Fretwork

Color comes as an unexpected jolt on this balcony in Virginia. The balustrate is Georgian fretwork.

Climate is another factor which has helped determine size and shape of windows. Harsh New England weather dictated small openings in the house shell, while Southern heat and humidity demanded taller, floor-to-ceiling windows that were as large as doors. In such near-tropical climes, the tall doors could be thrown open all around, inviting breezes indoors. Thus, the French door is the norm in many types of Southern regional architecture, especially in plantation houses.

Plains States

The great plains present a harmony of color: the weathered red barns framed by golden wheat fields.

Balconies

Flowerboxes on a second-floor balcony brighten the New Orleans street scene.

Here, the living areas are raised to the second level and shaded by wide roof overhangs that act as parasols to deflect heat off the windows.

Houses in the Far West have also evolved window treatments suited to that hot, dry climate. Adobe construction of thick clay walls proved to be an effective shelter against the desert conditions. The thick walls are heated by the sun all day and release that heat slowly at night when the temperatures often drop dramatically. Windows are

Victoriana

Typical Victorian windows are elongated and topped by an arch framed by the straight lintel.

Shadows

Shadows double the impression of a scalloped lintel on a Victorian cottage.

Colonial

Short and wide, the Colonial window is a double sash with symmetrical panes flanked by shutters.

Southwestern

Hatchwork from the plasterer's trowel patterns the walls of a Santa Fe adobe.

typically small and deeply set. They also are shaded by a roof extension that forms a continuous porch, called the portal. This not only acts as a sheltered walkway connecting the building's rooms, but also prevents the direct entry of searing sun and desert winds.

Like the human appendix, shutters are a rudiment from another time and have fallen into disuse. Octogenarians still remember, though, a daily chore they performed as children: in the winter when the sun went down at

French influence

Tall, floor-to-ceiling windows are part of the street scene in New Orleans.

Mediterranean

Rusticated walls and arches outlining these shuttered windows have a classical symmetry.

night, and in the summer when it became too hot, it was their task to run around the house to close all the window shutters. Window pane glass was notorious for transmitting heat. The shutters kept the sun's heat out at high noon and stopped its loss at night.

Today, shutters are purely decorative. Yet, they are so much a feature of particular period styles that most houses look denuded without them. There is a tendency to

White target

A bull's-eye painted white on the side of a barn is a target for the eye.

Durable

Shakes were so durable that houses from the 1700s still have their original shake siding.

remove the shutters from old houses when they are being painted—and not to put them back again. Because it is so difficult to locate original shutters (and shutter hardware), owners are far better off keeping their wood shutters in good repair. Once lost, they are almost impossible to replace.

Only in the 20th century has the view became the prime motive for window placement, although it was a consideration in Victorian times. Contemporary houses are specifically sited and

Country Victorian

The ornate lintels, turned brackets and drop finials bear testimony to America's architectural whimsy.

Regional Motifs

Folksy banisters developed according to the skill and whims of local carpenters.

Closed for Siesta

Towns in hot climates generally close down to escape the heat of the noonday sun. Hitching post has a horse head.

Cupolas

The tiny windows and crowning cupola are part of the American farm vernacular.

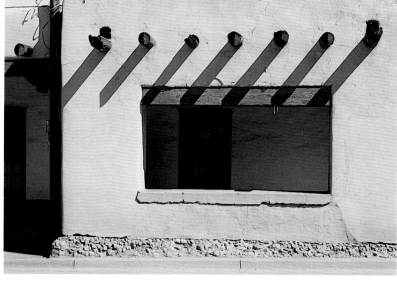

designed to concentrate on the best aspect of the view. A distant mountain range, a pond or lake, or any other pleasing vista determines both where to place the house on its site and where to put openings in the house envelope. The 20th century also marks the advent of the window comprising a single sheet of glass. This became possible only with air conditioning and central heating. Indeed, the technology that brought us insulating glass and the means to keep the house interior at a

Color Contrast

Stucco in sandy rose animates this Louisiana facade.

Picket Fence

The modern-day adaptation of the old fortress barricade, the picket fence is as American as apple pie.

comfortable temperature has drastically altered how our houses are built and what they look like. Once windows began to lose their role in temperature control, modern architecture went a step further in losing its regionalism—at a drastic expenditure of energy.

We are, however, beginning to work with nature once again, instead of disregarding her completely in house design. In the future we may see once again the strong regional differences in architecture that occurred in the past.

Exposed Beams

Vigas, or beams that extend past the stucco walls, are characteristic of adobe construction of the Southwest.

Flags Unfurled

A small town gears up for the Fourth of July parade with flags, bunting and striped window awnings.

Pathways express in eloquent terms the nation's technological and geographic progress. First came the simplest footpaths, a ribbon of green threading through the virgin forest. Sidewalks in small Colonial towns may have been brick lined, like those in Colonial Williamsburg. The first roads were gravel lanes traversed by horsedrawn carriages. And it wasn't

Footpaths

Early byways were often brick-lined. Other footpaths and streets were frequently made of cobblestones.

until the arrival of the automobile that paved thoroughfares became necessary and began to replace the quaint, if soggy, byways. The towns that developed alongside the new roads marked our westward expansion. These towns often had a regional spirit, especially in the early days. Thus, the towns of the Eastern Seaboard are Federal in character with their dignified architecture comprising straight lintels and door-

Roads

The nation's first roads were little more than gravel lanes that, in muddy weather, made travel arduous.

RAYMOND WAITES

RAYMOND WAITES

44

ways and simple lines. Travelling inward, the architecture of the mid-1800s changes to reflect the period of Midwest development, as buildings take on a Victorian air, with porches, gables, ornamented brackets and tall windows. The roadside architecture of the 20th century has a sadder record. Highways across the country are littered with fast-food signs and squat commercial buildings. We are losing the

Highways

Today, the country is crisscrossed by super highways, linking the coasts. One can traverse the country by car in a matter of days.

regionalism that makes our country so diverse and so endlessly fascinating. That's why it is so important to preserve and rehabilitate what little is left. Many do indeed appreciate how important their early architecture is: Providence, Baltimore, Newark, Portsmouth, Savannah, are all examples of towns that fought to reverse the slide into anonymity and turned slums into splendid historical sections.

Runways

In this age of supersonic travel, airplanes connect the four corners of the earth.

BARRY O'ROURKE/STOCK MARKET

MICHAEL SKOTT

BLUE DOOR
BLUE SKY

Blueberries, bluebells, blue eyes, cornflowers, blue jeans—blue is the favorite color of the majority of people. Perhaps it's because the two largest expanses of our world are blue: the blue sky and the blue oceans. In combination with white, blue is a dominant theme in the arts of many cultures. One need only think of the 18th-century Chinese export ware that is still avidly collected. In our own heritage, there is blue-and-white spatterware, homespun coverlets, and blue-and-white salt-glaze slipware. Blue is also special to Americans because it colors a corner of our flag. The uniforms of Yankee soldiers, you'll remember, were blue. In Colonial times, a house with a blue door meant that there were marriageable daughters dwelling inside. Blue has always been a color rich in historic associations. It's hard to go wrong with blue because there are few limitations in its use. Schemes that build on the blue spectrum tend to soothe and relax. Blue rooms, whether in the lighter hues or darker shades, are almost always inviting, sheltering, welcoming. Touch them with accents of pink and yellow and they really come alive.

BLUE

Market

FROM TRADITION

Have you ever wondered where pattern designs come from? Where, for instance, does a patterned fabric or wallpaper begin? Patterns do have starting points and rarely are they purely the imagination of their creators. Here, the Open Home Design Group assembled

Build a Theme

Assemble all the items you love and want to use—here, white china, blue-and-white fabrics, silver, and brass. It sets the mood of your room.

a group of shapes and objects that express a mood. In the detail below left, for instance, printed fabric is combined with other objects that share the same spirit; an old silver spoon, a bone-handled fork, and a china plate.

Already a mood has been established. The objects in the grouping express a certain feeling: 18th-century traditional style, like that of blue-and-white export china. These colors, patterns, and objects even dictate the kind

Take Inspiration

Often, a beautiful old fabric is an inspiration for color, style, and mood. This one was from the library at Fashion Institute of Technology, in New York.

TOM McCAVERA

TOM McCAVERA

50

of materials that go best with them.

This is not only how professional designers work, but how you also can design your rooms. Once the basic mood is set, you might look for patterns from history to adapt for today.

The documentary print of the flower was freely adapted into a wallpaper pattern. To coordinate with it, the designers created a geometric grid, or plaid, a tiny repeat floral, a larger geometric, and a medium-scale floral. With

Adapt if for Today

Patterns of grids, plaids, combine with florals in different scales. They all share compatible colors.

all their diversity, the patterns are unified by the basic blue-and-white color theme.

At this point, we can return to the beginning of the process to see how the new coordinates work alongside the old textiles. The detail, below right, provides the answer. An early American homespun, it blends beautifully with all of the other fabrics on this page.

Think Texture

An antique homespun fabric from Colonial days shares the same spirit as the contemporary patterns beside it.

TOM McCAVERA

TOM McCAVERA

NEW FROM OLD

Blue-and-white is one of the world's favorite color combinations. Through the ages, we find it in the designs of many cultures. That's why the Open Home Design Group selected it as the starting point for this new collection of fabrics and wallpapers. When blue mixes with other colors, see the rich palette that results.

One of blue's most beautiful natural complements is red. Not the hot red of a firecracker but the toned-down red of oxblood stain on painted furniture, or the red of an old barn. That combination occured in a historic fabric, below right. The fabric is lovely paired with touches of brass, stripped pine, and dried flowers.

That multi-colored documentary print is seen translated into contemporary wallpaper patterns and then

TOM McCAVERA

TOM McCAVERA

matched up with borders. Notice how the difference in the background tones changes the mood of the same design. In the darker version, the mood is rich, atmospheric, sumptuous. In the version with a cream-colored background, the same design is light-hearted, fresh, playful.

Those same mood changes would happen in a room using these patterns. The darker the pattern's coloration, the deeper and more atmospheric the

Add a Border

Borders for wallpaper are enjoying renewed popularity. They were also favored in Victorian times.

resulting room. While the same pattern with a lighter ground would make the room feel lighter and airier. Remember, dark colors tend to enclose a space. Lighter tones brighten it up and make it feel sunnier.

The way patterns can be combined to accentuate a color theme is seen below right. Here, a plaid mixes compatibly with florals in medium- and small-scaled designs. Imagine what a charming room they would create.

Think Blue

The blue color field bonds this spirited mix of plaids, repeats, and multi-colored florals.

TOM McCAVERA

TOM McCAVERA

NEW TRADITION

When you have determined the mood you want your room to have, you're ready to select the blue that best expresses it. A desire for drama might lead into the deeper end of the blue spectrum, such as the navy tones or rich, regal blue. The darker the color, the deeper the drama. And, curiously, many people respond to these color-saturated shades. Wallpapers with a deep blue background are the

Mix it up

Compatible colors link "Gingham Plaid" with "Colony Quilt," a dot repeat, and "Nosegay," a medium-scale floral. A solid fabric, "Admiral," is used for accent. All are from the Open Home collection.

Paint it blue

Blue and white is still the hands-down favorite. Here, the white oculus stands out against blue siding.

TOM McCAVERA

JOHN EARLE /STOCK MARKET

best selling of any other color. Deep blue, with its associations of night and ocean blue, must fill a need in our psyche.

Lighter blues, on the other hand, result in rooms that are brighter and fresher in feeling. Blues that are tinged with red move into the purple family—with all of the fragile tones of lilac and mauve. These are chamelion colors, neither blues nor reds, that are lovely in places, like the bedroom, where soft color is soothing.

Mixing pattern with pattern is a trend that is growing. And, there is a

Alternate prints

Two prints combine in a room: beneath the chair rail is "Gingham Plaid" wallpaper; above it is "Rosebud" a small, floral repeat.

simple formula for combining them successfully. As you select patterns, choose only one of the three basic types. They are a grid, such as a plaid or stripe, a small-scale repeat like that of a polka dot or small floral that looks like one, and a larger-scale floral. All of these should be related in color. This really is the most basic pattern mix. And, it nearly always results in handsome rooms by virtue of the color bond.

Color provides the underlying unity that blends the patterns together. In the details, below, you see how and why it works.

Update the Old

The classic wing chair gets a whole new look when the sides are panelled in wood. It's part of the Open Home collection.

TOM McCAVERA

TOM McCAVERA

Buy an Armoire

This is Open Home's commodious storage for the TV, hi-fi, or just about anything. The warm pine wood repeats the wood of the wing chair and floor.

Mix Three Prints

The sofa itself combines the three basic prints: a small floral is "Pot Pourri" the overall fabric; accent pillows mix "Rosebud," a small scale print and "Rose Border," a large floral, repeated on the sofa's skirt.

Voguewright Studio

LIVING WITH BLUE AND PINE

Blue is such a relaxing color that one can safely use a lot of it in a room. Here, for instance, shades of blue and pattern coordinates are used on all of the upholstered furniture. This is what the Open Home Design Group envisioned as they created the prints we have seen on preceding pages. Here, again, is the basic pattern mix we advocate: a grid, a small-scale repeat and a large floral. These are used with the texture of the rag rug and the warm woodtones of natural pine. The design principles we have explained to you on page 12 and 13 have come home in this invitingly livable room.

TOM McCAVERA

Mix a Dot and Grid

The two occasional chairs sport two other important pattern types: one lounge chair wears "Rosebud," a dot repeat; the other, "Colony Plaid," a basic grid pattern.

Allow Clutter

This room's inviting quality comes from its comfortable clutter: a wreath in the making; sofa pillows as seats on the floor, magazines ready to read. It's a room that looks—and is—lived in.

57

DINING WITH BLUE

Parties are the perfect excuse to experiment with new ways to present food and to play with color on the table. Let everything on the table contribute to a convivial spirit and festive mood. Using plates and napkins in two different colors is a good way to start. It limits the elements of your setting to two basic hues, which are repeated elsewhere, as in the little flower baskets used as centerpieces.

Echo the Centerpiece

Yet one more way to present the napkin: roll it up and place it in a napkin ring, then string tiny flowers and buds through the ring. These should be a small place-setting version of the larger table centerpiece.

Make Color a Theme

Once the color scheme is set you can reinforce it in many ways. Here, even the party favors are wrapped in the same colors of pink and blue. Set at each place, these become visual treats for the eye as well as gifts for the guests. They're guaranteed to please.

Alternate Color

Vary the table by alternating two sets of colorful plates. The pink plate gets the blue napkin at one place setting; the blue plate takes the pink napkin.

Try the Unusual

The conventional way to serve breads and rolls is in a basket inset with a napkin. Try this for an inventive variation: Wrap the bread in a colorful napkin so it nestles in the folds. Add a flower sprig for visual garnish. The result is an unexpected surprise that's sure to charm your guests and liven up the table.

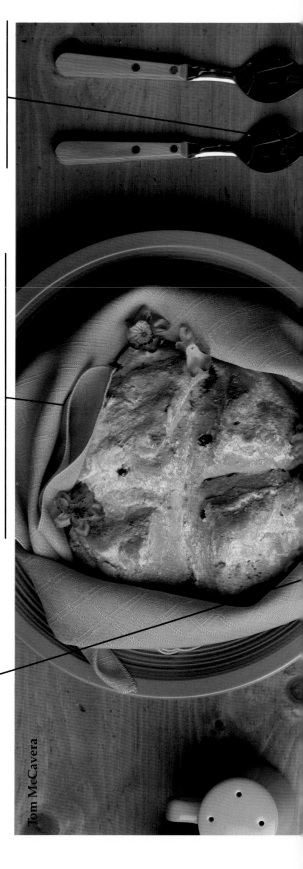

Tom McCavera

DRESSING A DOOR

Special occasions are the perfect time to dress up the house. At holiday times, especially, a joyful spirit suffuses the entire house and familiar rooms take on a festive air. We want the rooms, filled with family and guests, to express our happiness. Christmas, Thanksgiving, birthdays, weddings—all are reasons to rejoice.

The conventional way to decorate for important times is, of course, with flowers. Use flowers in unexpected

Gather the Greens

The first step in making a garland is gathering the materials: You'll need lots of one variety for the base. From the fields in Haverhill, New Hampshire, Amy chose armfuls of goldenrod and ironweed. For accent, she picked red zinnias from the garden. When you collect your own flowers, remember that the base flowers must have long stems. You'll also need a spool of florists' wire or picture-frame wire.

Fasten them Together

Begin by looping the wire around a handful of goldenrod stems. Do not cut the wire. Continue to lap more flowers on top of the first ones in regular intervals. Use the flower heads as your guide. Lap them so that the flowers you're adding lie just beneath the heads of those already fastened with wire. Keep twining the wire around the flower stems only, so that the wire forms a lengthening spiral around the stems as you progress. Lay the lengthening garland flat on the ground because it's easier to work that way. When the garland is the right length, cut the wire. Now the garland can be studded with zinnias and other flowers.

RAYMOND WAITES

RAYMOND WAITES

arrangements and places. There are many more ways to work with flowers than simply placing them in a vase. Wreaths, garlands and spectacular centerpieces are remarkably easy to make. All it entails is a fertile imagination— and armfuls of plant materials. Because flowers are expensive when you purchase them at a florist, look around you to see what nature has to offer. Fields and meadows abound in flowers. At most times of the year, something is blooming bountifully. Goldenrod, black-eyed Susans, Queen Anne's lace, chicory, field daisies, purple loosestrife, lupine, and beautiful grasses grow like weeds in summer and fall. Autumn also brings branches of colorful leaves, such as scarlet sugar maple, yellow poplar, rust oak, and vivid red sumac. Winter, while less verdant, provides fir boughs, holly, pine cones, pyracantha and other bright berries. In the South, nothing is more magnificent than the huge, glossy leaves of the magnolia tree. Use them all. Just how easy it is to make a garland from native greens is shown here, where Amy Wrapp assembled one for a bright blue door. It took about two hours to complete.

Hang the Garland

The completed garland was fastened to the doorframe with nails at each top corner and in the center. Wire was threaded through the garland and looped around the nailheads. A colorful garland makes a doorway a joyous sight.

MICHAEL SKOTT

Mirror on Pegs

The simple technique of placing pegs all around the room unites all the hanging objects in a common design theme. Use pegs to hang a mirror.

Lilo Raymond

Blue Stain

Muted color provided the Shaker interior with an accent that was never discordant or jarring. These subtle wood stains are equally appealing and useful in today's rooms.

Fabric

Collectors prize Shaker fabrics and textiles as much as their furniture. We can hardly wonder at this when we see these marvelously subtle designs.

A Traditional Style

Fishermen once made bed canopies in their spare time, using the same techniques they used to make fish nets. Netted canopies are beautiful, and modern versions can be purchased today.

An American Art

Quiltmaking was a way for frugal pioneer women to use fabric scraps. They traded pieces of gingham and cotton from cast-off clothes to gain the right colors and textures. Thus developed the intricate and original designs of traditional American quilts. Beautiful quilts like this one are still being made from old patterns.

FISHNET CANOPY

Canopy beds were originally draped, and developed out of the need to keep in heat and dispel drafts in damp stone castles. Trapping heat was still a factor in early New England homes. In the South, though, bed curtains were more effective for keeping out insects. Today, with improved windows and screens, bed canopies are purely decorative. But the magical memory of the early draped bed lingers on, and canopy beds have an irresistible appeal.

Stencil a Floor

Stenciling the floor
highlights the hearth
and puts an elegant
border all around the
room.

Use Armoires

Older homes are notoriously short on closets. The renewed popularity of the armoire with its roomy interiors is a boon to homeowners who lack storage closets.

Michael Skott

RAG RUGS

The standard covering for floors in Colonial times was the rag rug. Today's versions, like the one from Op Home, come many colors.

Leave Out a Doll

Little girls aren't the only ones who still love dolls; grown-ups do, too. Leave your favorite Raggedy Ann out where it will make you smile every time you see it.

STRIPES AND LACE

Bedrooms are the perfect places to indulge in decorating whimsy. In our personal retreats we can give free rein to all the special things we love. Canopy beds and Raggedy Anns, frills, ruffles, and fluffy pillows, favorite photographs and pretty quilts—all of these romantic elements are at home in the bedroom. It is, after all, our only truly personal fantasy space.

Indulge Yourself

A sky-blue bedspread and ruffled canopy echo the blue in the striped wallpaper. You can buy all of the furniture and bed clothes from Open Home.

Hang Old Lace

Antique lace hung like a painting will add a subtle textural contrast to your wall. And it adds a delicate note to any room.

Turn Back the Bed

Frilly eyelet borders the bed sheets and dust ruffle. If you keep the sheets turned back, you can enjoy the lacy look during the day as well as at night.

MICHAEL SKOTT

69

DINING IN BLUE

Many shades of blue combine with reproduction furniture and folk objects to give this dining room a special country modern ambiance. Walls are a soft teal blue, draperies an even softer sky blue heightened by their translucency. The hooked rug, a modern design influenced by antique rugs, picks up all the blue values. The furniture and the hooked rug in this room are pieces you can purchase. They are part of Open Home.

Grapevine Garland

Use wreaths as festive keynotes when you entertain. An unadorned grapevine wreath can change with seasons. Here, the basic wreath is studded with zinnias in a celebration of summer blooms.

Ladderback Chairs

Antique ladderback chairs are expensive. Reproductions are just as charming and work equally well. Sears sells these ladderbacks as part of its Open Home collection.

70

Bountiful Bouquet

When planning a table centerpiece, look at what's blooming outside. This bountiful bouquet is made of goldenrod and ironweed, mixed with red and pink zinnias from the garden.

Think Big

If your decoration consists of field flowers, use armfuls. Fill a large basket or wooden bowl until it's brimming over for a really spectacular display.

MICHAEL SKOTT

71

Restore Historic Details

This unusual mural was painted around 1834 by Rufus Porter, a popular muralist of the time. Itinerant painters traveled around seeking commissions, such as this one, to decorate walls in private homes. The mural's subject is the nearby White Mountains of New Hampshire. The broken limb symbolized a recent death in the family.

Accent the Natural

Used in combination with the wood blinds, the softly looped tiebacks and full folds of the light blue draperies underscore the natural color scheme.

HIDDEN GEM

The many hues of blue bring calmness to this dining room. The blue mural, which covers the room's four walls, has mellowed with age. The woodwork is painted a soft teal blue. But these quiet shades work nicely with the room's modern colors, such as the brighter blue of the table linens and the blue accent in the hooked rug.

Use Modern Versions of Old Things

Wood venetian blinds, a feature from Colonial days, cast a warm glow in this room. They were also used in Independence Hall in Philadelphia.

Think Simple

The charm of this ladderback chair is its utter simplicity. The blinds, draperies, and chair are all from the Open Home collection.

Michael Skott

73

PINK HOUSE
ROSE BUDS

Pink ribbons, peonies, piglets, and valentines. Rose and pink are the prettiest colors in nature's palette. Driving down a country road, you'll smile when you come upon a pink house. Nearly all towns seem to have one. Some unpainted adobe buildings in the Southwest and in Louisiana actually take on a shade of dusty rose when tinted by sunshine, since rose is the natural color of certain types of stucco. No longer regarded as strictly feminine colors, muted rose and pink are part of our visual vocabulary, and are being used more freely in the home. Rooms benefit from all the newly popular rose tones and their relatives in the color family: peach, apricot, melon, and terracotta. These tones are flattering to both the room and its occupants. The rosy hues send off a lightness that is livable—and romantic. Rose and its color family are superb mixers. Pink and white is certainly one of the prettiest combinations. But pink also works amicably with all the other pastels, as well as with more subtle naturals, such as stripped pine and even furniture painted in deeper tones, such as those verging on brick and barn red.

Raymond Waites

**AMERICAN
ROSE**

A bee's-eye view
of the rosebud
shows its sen-
sual shades of
pinks in all their
glory.

Put up a Shelf

Look overhead when you need additional storage. Here, a bookshelf was installed along the window's top edge.

Gather Blossoms

Flowers are an excellent way to introduce a burst of color into a neutral scheme. Part of the beauty is that they can change with the seasons, and even from day to day.

78

BURST OF COLOR

The soothing feel of this study is the result of the room's mellow wood tones. It is a room that defies labeling as either contemporary or traditional. When designer John Saladino converted this guest cottage into a study, he carefully matched any new elements to the room's existing architectural features, such as the pine-panelled walls. Above all, the design illustrates how easy naturals are to live with, for this is a room meant for introspection, contemplation, and pleasure.

Keep it Natural

The new casement windows are left in their natural state rather than painted or stained.

Bring in Accents

An antique wood trough filled with green apples adds subtle color. The items like the chess set become three-dimensional patterns in this serene space.

Use Antiques

An antique Windsor chair lends special grace and mellow tones to the room.

DINING WITH ROSE

Many of us are far too timid when it comes to setting the table. With the wealth of tablewares on the market, composing the table is far simpler than it seems. Here, the pattern of the pink floral dishes sets the theme, and the floral pink-on-pink statement is repeated in all the accessories. Pink and white with splashes of yellow also play a key role in this table's winning composition. Afternoon tea, complete with cookies, croissants, and lemon slices delight the eye and whet the appetite.

Key the Flowers

Even the choice of flowers is keyed to the arrangement. Yellow miniature mums encircle a pink carnation as a miniature posy between place settings.

Mix Dried Flowers

When it's impossible to get fresh flowers, you can use dried ones and still capture the feeling of fresh. (Do avoid plastic flowers.) Studding paper flowers with babies'-breath and gingham ribbons makes a charming centerpiece.

Tom McCavera

80

RE-THINKING PINK

This table setting exemplifies how new patterns are translated from historic ones. The cabbage rose motif of the tablecloth's border is a contemporary interpretation of the same documentary print that you saw on page 52. The dishes echo a blue-and-white export ware but worked in a tone-on-tone color palette. The Open Home Design Group used such documentary prints when developing the designs pictured here. The things of the past inspire objects for today's living.

Add a Wood Touch

Wood-handled flatware brings in warm wood tones. These are dishwasher-proof.

Build on a Color

A solid colored napkin reinforces the basic pink scheme. It's "Windowpane"; dishes are "Chintz Dusty Rose" pattern; all by the Open Home Design Group.

Coordinate Linens

Pink cabbage roses bordering the tablecloth echo the roses of the patterned dish. Such play of pattern on pattern gives the table a light-hearted romance.

81

LIVING WITH ROSE

Color is the underlying bond that unites different patterns and prints. When you begin to work out a color scheme, select the shade of rose or pink that you find particularly appealing. You'll often find it in a fabric or a wallpaper pattern, but it may also come from a rug or a painting that you already have. Using a wallpaper as the starting point, though,

Paint the House

It's daring, but painting the house pink changes its whole personality. Choose the softest, most subtle shade for a house exterior.

does have an advantage. Its tones have already been chosen to work together, so you can use them as a basis for the color design of your room.

Once you've established your basic color scheme, other patterns and tones can be blended with it. Bear in mind that there is a simple way to work with pattern. It is this: choose one from each of three types: a grid, a small-scale print, and a floral. By playing with different scales of these patterns, the room will have visual interest.

If you study the mix of prints in the

Try for Harmonies

When mixing patterns think about design harmonies. A small berry print is a good choice for walls or upholstery.

LILO RAYMOND

TOM McCAVERA

Blend in Florals

Consider scale as you blend in florals with geometrics. Choose one that's larger than your smaller berry print.

Work out a scheme

In the detail below, the Open Home designers played large scale against small; coordinating them with solid color, a plaid and dotted grid. Note how well they look against natural pine wood tones.

detail below, you can visualize how a pattern mix develops. There is a grid (or plaid), and a small-scale floral, worked against a solid color and larger floral.

Once your patterns are set, you can try them out with other elements that you plan to use. The last picture is a photograph of an armoire, taken from a magazine. It's obvious that stripped pine would be a welcome addition to this rose-toned scheme. Think about all of the other accessories that would enliven the room, such as white ironstone, country furniture and baskets.

Clip Magazines

A picture of an armoire was cut out of a magazine and laid alongside the pattern choices. Use strings of yarn in bright tones to try out possible accent colors.

RAYMOND WAITES

83

FOR A ROSE MOOD

We've already seen on the preceding page how color and pattern work together. Now we can see how they translate into furnishings for the home. The sheets, table settings, dishes, and even rag rugs are all related in color scheme.

Patterns often come in both "positive" and "negative" versions of an identical print, which simplifies design decisions. In the bedroom detail below left, for instance, one basic pattern is used. But in each version, the colors are reversed. One print has the rose tone as its background; in the reverse version, the background is white and the berry tone is picked up as the pattern. Using the same pattern in its two versions makes coordinating them in a scheme easy.

When you go out to purchase furnishings for your rooms, bear in mind the color relationships of the objects and fabrics. In these details, for instance, the rose and blue tones are the

Reverse the Patterns

Berry-toned sheets in reverse patterns contribute to this bed's charm. The wallpaper coordinates with one of the prints. The pattern is "Sweet William" from the Open Home collection.

Borrow from Nature

A flaming azalea bush heralds spring. Note how it echoes the color of the house's roof.

TOM McCAVERA

BOB WOODWARD/STOCK MARKET

84

base colors. All of the other colors either mix or contrast with them. In the table setting, lighter patterned placemats pick up the two basic tones. Dishes play against those tones while the napkins bring in color contrasts.

Notice how natural things spark the whole palette. Eggs in a brightly colored bowl are natural components of the scheme, intensifying all the color. Flowers enrich the hues, adding their lively tones to the solids and patterns.

In the detail, below right, we see colors building upon each other in the selection of rag rugs. All of the rugs

Underscore the Setting

Choose placemats that repeat the color of your dishes. Then build on that color with contrasting and matching napkins.

share a muted palette. They are almost sherbet-colored pastels, taken from the flower colors but muted and softened by white. The subtle striations come from the texture and materials of the rugs themselves.

The nubby texture of the rugs is a pleasing contrast to other materials one would use in a room. Picture one of these lovely pastel-toned rugs used in the bedroom with the sheets we've just described. Texture, pattern, and color play are the building blocks of any design scheme. The most beautiful rooms are built on the interplay.

Bring in Texture

The nubby texture in this array of rag rugs is what's needed underfoot in many rooms. All the furnishings here are from Open Home.

TOM McCAVERA

TOM McCAVERA

85

NEW AND OLD

Once upon a time this soft pastel was relegated to the child's bedroom. Now, pinks are recognized as sophisticated tones that are particularly versatile and easy to live with. The power of pink, like that of other pastels, is that it does not overpower a space but casts a rosy glow throughout. The prettiest accent is still white, which complements and plays up the richness of pink.

Textural Play

Ironstone and white china are perfect touches to use with pink. The textural play of shiny smooth china against soft fabrics and patterned wallpaper is particularly pleasing.

Divide a Door

The double Dutch door was a familiar feature of Colonial houses. This Dutch door divides a closet, which is fitted out to store linens and china. The best part about it is that, while the top stores items used all the time, the bottom portion can store little-used items, and furniture can be placed against it.

Add a Modern Accent

An easy way to add modern flavor to the older home is to cover the walls in a geometric grid wallpaper. Here, the sprightly geometric design is an upbeat touch in a period room.

New Versions of Old

These plates are contemporary versions of old spatterware. Our forebears would be surprised to see them here reproduced in shocking pink.

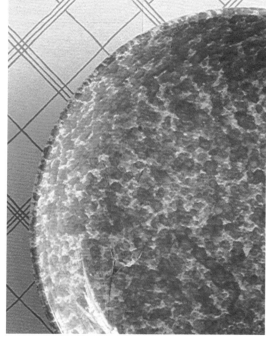

MICHAEL SKOTT

87

Attend Auctions

Vesta Smith bought this old quilt at auction for $2. It has one ragged edge that she tucks up so it doesn't show.

Make the New from the Old

Many contemporary prints take their design cues from old patterns. Sheets in the "Sweet William" pattern are an example. The comforter, too, is new: "Pamela" from the Open Home collection.

MICHAEL SKOTT

ROSY BEDROOM

The essence of country-style decorating is a mix of traditional objects with colors and patterns that share the same spirit. In Vesta Smith's bedroom in New Hampshire, for instance, a patchwork quilt, hung on the wall, combines with ironstone, an antique rocking horse and painted country chairs. Fabrics, wallpaper, and bed linens are modern designs but reminiscent of the past. This is what's meant by taking your cue from country objects and building a decorating scheme around them.

Sponge-paint a Wall

Vesta Smith had the lower part of the wall hand-painted in a modern version of old sponge-painting. The color is picked up from the wallpaper.

Brighten the Floor

Our Colonial ancestors painted their floors to add color—a good idea that works equally well in today's homes. Light floor colors make dark rooms seem brighter.

Paint Country Chairs

Little country chairs like this one are still available at good prices. Just paint them in a new color to match your scheme. Bed, nightstand, and lamp are new and from the Open Home collection.

ROSE ON ROSE

PINK ON PINK

The pink rug was the starting point for this bedroom's color scheme. The room's rosy wall was painted to match the rug's background hue.

Be Unconventional

To double the color impact, throw a small rug on top of a larger one. Who says it shouldn't be done!

ROSE FINALE

K ACCENT

arming col-
on of barn
als fills
ooks and
nies of this
nsical room.
bright pink
e paper fan
the punch
lor.

PINE CONES
FIELD FLOWERS

Seashells, baskets, old wood beams, homespun linens and muslin, stripped pine. Naturals are all around us. They are familiar, warm, and evocative of bygone times when everything was made by hand. Natural things bring texture and character to a color scheme. They also soften and smooth the hard edges of modern spaces. Naturals are foolproof for color schemes. They provide a neutral background for the livelier colors, blending and balancing the brighter hues, and thereby intensifying their beauty. The most humble objects, a collection of pine cones or a bowl of seashells, for instance, lend a subtle gradation of tone to a room. Use pine furniture with stucco and plaster and watch its mellow warmth permeate your entire scheme. White, too, creates the most sophisticated of rooms. White-on-white used as a no-color scheme where all of the fabrics and furnishings are white continues to be the favorite choice for many people. New England towns where all the houses and the village church are white are a cherished part of our American architectural heritage. White and naturals together are exceedingly versatile. They go with anything.

NATURALS

NATURALS C. 1650

**OD AND
TE**

 subtle inter-
of warm
l tones
ist white
er is part of
eauty of
enturies-
arn.

Michael Skott

Whimsy

This enchanting farm-
stead illustrates the
playfulness of Amer-
ica's builders. It sits on
a street in Monroe,
Michigan, amidst
more recent—and
much more serious—
neighboring houses.

Riotous Trim

Wood carvings for
house trim ran the riot
of scallops and curli-
cues around the turn
of the century. Here,
the scalloped trim ani-
mates the porch; its
lacy edge contrasts
sharply with the
pointed picket fence.

WHITE PICKET FENCE

Howard Kaplan

Light and Air

Coming from industrialized Manchester, Mother Ann advocated fresh air and ventilation—hence the large, uncurtained windows of Shaker buildings.

Ingenious Storage

Shakers hung chairs on pegs around the room so the space could be effectively swept, and to leave room for the "shaking" or dancing that played a role in their religious ritual.

Superb Craftsmanship

Shaker chairs are masterpieces of delicate proportions and comfort. Since there was no decoration to hide flaws, the workmanship had to be perfect.

Spare and Pure

Shaker furniture is exceptionally clean and elegant in line. It looks surprisingly modern.

Old Porch Rocker

Rockers were a uniquely American development. Not only the Shakers made them, so did other country craftsmen. The Brumby rocker, shown here, is still a fixture on front porches.

SIMPLE AND EASY

Shakers regarded work as a form of worship. This religious community was founded by Mother Ann Lee, who, in 1774, left Manchester, England on the *Mariah* with eight followers. At its height, there were 18 Shaker colonies with about 6,000 members. They were superb artisans, and furniture making was their chief industry. By 1830, Shaker-made chairs and rockers were sought after as the finest seating made in America.

BOB WOODWARD/STOCK MARKET

103

SEASHORE COLORS

This dining room's color scheme of warm naturals with black accents, was inspired by two elements: seashells from nearby beaches and wooden decoys. Located on Figure Eight Island, North Carolina, this weekend house belongs to Ben and Bonnie Helms, both incurable collectors. Bonnie picks up shells off the beaches, and Ben collects wooden decoys from local antique shops. The colors of these "finds" are especially important to them, so much so that they asked Raymond Waites to create a room around the natural colors seen in their collections. The new items they continue to acquire simply enhance the room.

Use Black for Contrast

Until Ben finds the additional antique chairs he's searching for—like the one in the foreground—the handsome antique table is surrounded by inexpensive chairs that have been stained black. The pickled white floor, expertly done to let the grain show through, offers a clean, fresh counterpoint to the mellow old pine table and arm chairs. The black side chairs provide a dramatic contrast.

Display Your Treasure

The open shelves, pickled white, are an excellent foil for the colors of the pottery and jugs, and make a super showcase for the unusual shapes of the wooden decoys.

Mix Different Styles

A single antique chair is easy to find. A matched set is much rarer—and expensive. Remember that chairs don't have to match. This antique arrowback armchair is used with Windsor reproductions. The copies come in natural wood; here they have been stained to give them the look of greater age.

WHISICAL

Country furniture is probably one of the most popular of today's decorating choices. And no wonder. It takes the anonymity out of modern, unimaginative spaces and gives rooms warmth and style. There are many ways to design around country pieces, and we see the best in this charming dining room in a California house: All of the furniture is large in scale, rustic woods are mixed with painted pieces, and toys add humorous accents.

Elyse Lewin

Be Bold

A large part of this room's country charm stems from the fanciful accessories. The toy horse is really too big for the table top. But it is exactly its bold size that makes it work.

Repeat the Color

Color is used judiciously to complement all the rustic wood tones. The blue-and-white rug repeats the room's other blue accents, such as the painted chest beneath the window.

Accent with Art

Antique portraits have lots of character. The pose of the body and expression of the face add intrigue to the space.

106

Let Your Taste be Your Guide

Turn-of-the-century flatware like this three-pronged fork can still be found. Don't let the fact that it can't go into a dishwasher deter you from buying and using it.

A Spontaneous Touch

The most casual flower arrangement can be elegant. Toss a bunch of narcissus in an old canning jar. This unstudied arrangement adds a personal accent to your table.

A NATURAL WAY TO ENTERTAIN

When designer Raymond Waites and his wife, Nancy, entertain, Nancy cooks and Raymond adds the finishing touches to the table. They rarely set the table in the same way twice. First, they decide on the menu, and then they delve into the cornucopia of tablewares that they have collected over the years. For a party in their country home in East Hampton, Long Island, the setting might include earthenware plates they found in New Mexico, an eclectic mix of flatware, and napkins made from mattress ticking. "At first, Nancy's mother was shocked because nothing matched," said Raymond. "But we love to collect things and we want to use them all."

Use What You Have

Don't worry if you have a set of antique spoons but no matching forks or knives. Use them anyway. These heirloom spoons belonged to Nancy's grandmother. Their owners' pride and joy, she mixes them here with flea market silverplate knives and horn-handled forks.

Look for Good Buys

An old railway bench, the kind found in waiting rooms of small-town train stations, makes a fine dining room settle. This one came from The Wrecking Bar in Atlanta and, in 1982, cost less than $100. Great buys can still be found by the scavenger with a sophisticated eye.

Collect on Vacation

Traveling often turns up unusual things for the table. These earthenware plates were found on a trip through New Mexico at a craftsman's pottery shop.

Simple Chairs

Like tableware, seating is more interesting when it doesn't match. Rush-seated Mexican chairs cost $25 when purchased in 1964 and are still sold in stores today. But they are more expensive. (That's inflation.)

WHITE ON WHITE

White, though considered a "non-color," can actually be one of the most powerful elements in a color scheme. Because white is the absence of color, it can be the easiest "color" to design with. First of all, it doesn't clash with other colors, but acts as a perfect foil for them, letting them take center stage. And if you tire of your decor, you merely have to change the color of the accessories to have a fresh look.

The better you understand how white behaves, the more success you'll have working with it. Remember, it is the absence of color, so if you need the warmth color provides, you must add

Bleach them White

What could look more luxurious than stacks of thick white towels, and what could be more practical? No sorting required, simply toss in the bleach and do a full load. Here, necklaces hung on the antique shelf and rod, provide the color in the otherwise all-white scheme.

warm neutrals or at least a few splashes of a warm color. White tends to visually enlarge a space so if that's your goal, you're on the right track in choosing it. As a background, white allows attention to be focussed on the furnishings, so it's perfect when you're ready to show everything off in its final glory.

Used properly, there is no denying that the white scheme is highly sophisticated. It's a favorite among people who have art collections to display. It is dramatic when used with black, gray, or another neutral and punctuated with one vibrant color. It is heaven-sent for energy-conscious people, since it makes it easier and less expensive to light a room. And it is widely embraced by people in dense urban areas because of the brightness it brings to where there is none. White deck-floors, for instance, give instant vitality to a room.

MICHAEL SKOTT

BARRY O'ROURKE/STOCK MARKET

110

Show It Off

Create a focal point with a display of all-white objects. It could be china, paper-weights, antique white glass candle-holders, or even ceramic mugs. Choose the background to create the mood you want. Here it's natural wood, but paint, fabric, wallcovering, or cork are appropriate alternatives.

Use Contrast

Though these ironstone aspic molds are, in essence, all white, there are subtle variations in their colorings. In this marvelous mix each one gains in importance. The contrast of shapes, sizes, colors, and textures will give distinction to each piece in your collection.

White upholstered furniture is unquestionably elegant. Needless to say, white is also perishable—particularly on furniture. Fortunately slipcovers are back in vogue, and *de rigueur* if there are pets, children, or feet-up types in the family. Surprisingly, slightly battered white slipcovers have a unique appeal—sort of an elegant shabbiness. Laundering them just seems to add to their style. English country manor houses all have that appeal—of slipcovers worn thin by wear.

Because of its versatility, white mixes with everything. Often people who work around color all day need the restful repose of an all-white room to come home to. White environments are cool, congenial, reflective, timeless. Best of all, they never seem to go out of style.

Add Vibrancy

White is forceful. It visually pushes any color near it forward, giving color greater intensity. See how important the white razors, ointment jars and other small objects appear against a white background.

MICHAEL SKOTT

111

NATURE'S BOUNTY

Even the most casual supper for family or close friends can be festive. Arrange the setting around the preparation and presentation of the meal and have everyone join in the chopping and garnishing of the foods at table. Take the vegetables out of their paper bags and put them into pretty bowls. Condiments, too, and even the kitchen utensils should be part of your arrangement. Make a simple meal an occasion.

Visual Tableaux

Vary the shape and color of the bowls for foods and condiments to create a still-life composition that takes the place of a center-piece. Fresh ingredients look especially appetizing when served in good-looking pottery.

Atmosphere

Decant the wine into a colorful crock to let it air and to enhance its bouquet. Use candles at evening meals to shed a soft, romantic light.

Seasonal Setting

Coordinate your table setting with the season. In wintry weather, surround the dinner plates with fir branches instead of placemats.

TV STYLE

Television (and all its add-on equipment) has changed our lives. Meals often end up eaten in front of the TV. Dining on a tray by the couch in order to catch your favorite television show makes the most of a solitary meal. It works equally well for two—or four—when the evening's event is staying home to catch an old movie or watch a new one on the VCR.

Get Comfortable

Dining alone needn't be dreary when dinner time comes along. This is the time to experiment with tablewares and to see what mixes well together. And don't forget style just because you're alone—arrange your dinner tray as attractively as you would when expecting important guests.

ROBERT GRANT

NATURALS: BASKETS

Dine by Candlelight

An 18th-century chandelier is sometimes better than one that's electrified. The table is bathed in candle glow.

Concentrate on Form

Folk-art objects make delightful substitutes for paintings when hung on the wall.

Elyse Lewin

Vary Shapes

A cheese basket lends its rich texture to the overhead composition.

Hang Baskets

Baskets look so friendly when hung up in clusters from old beams.

Mix the Textures

Baskets come in so many great varieties that mixing splint, rush, and woven ones always works textural magic.

NATURALS: RESTFUL

RESTFUL

A guest cottage in Connecticut blends new features in with the old.

MICHAEL SKOTT

Light Creatively

A musician's cymbal makes an elegant lamp. Hung from the ceiling, it does away with the need for a bedside lamp on a night table.

Re-use Old Doors

The designer utilized old doors and patterned the new one after them. Antique hardware unites the old and new.

Install a Window

A small window gives a house guest a tree-top view from the sleeping loft.

Add a Loft

To fit a new bathroom into his guest cottage, designer John Saladino sectioned off a part of the bedroom. But he had the new wall plastered to match the existing ones. A bonus: the loft bed over the new bathroom.

Michael Skott

WHITE-ON-WHITE
The power of this sturdy old barn, reconstructed piece by-piece on Long Island, dictates the few large-scale pieces of furniture. Sofas covered in white seem to float in the enveloping space.

DAFFODILS
COPPER KETTLES

Yellow lemons, green limes, buttercups with green stems, honeybees, golden eggs. Yellow is a happy color that has many personalities. Sometimes it's pale as the sand and wheat fields; other times it's brassy as a new penny. All of the sunny tones from daffodils to brass are warming influences in spaces. When you want to up the sunlight in a dark room, paint it yellow. In fact, rooms that face north and feel cold regardless of the weather will take on the temperature of a southern exposure. Paint the kitchen ceiling yellow and it is almost as effective at bringing in the sun as installing a skylight. In nature, yellow often comes paired with green. That's probably why this combination turns up so often in rooms, too. But the duo works best when one or the other is toned down. Bright yellow and bright green are too much competition for a single interior space. Whether you specifically choose yellow as the color base of your design scheme or not, you can't help using it. Yellow tones are present in many natural things, such as stripped pine and other wood grains, as well as in metals like copper and brass. Keep that in mind.

YELLOW AND GREEN

Raymond Waites

YELLOW SURPRISE

Barry Elz/Stock Market

**NATURAL
YELLOW**

...umn creates
...or sensation
...llows, reds
...greens. Na-
...s yellow is
...ed on a barn
...e Catskill
...ntains of
...York State.

SHAKER YELLOW

The Shakers used utilitarian objects to enliven their rooms. These simple, elegant items give the Shaker interior an overall sense of calm and order. Yet while understatement is the keynote, these rooms are by no means dull. They are indeed examples of the vibrancy that can come from simplicity.

Hang Pegs

The practical Shakers hung nearly everything on pegs attached to boards on the walls. The pegs varied in length: narrow objects were hung on short pegs, but wider ones, like this kettle, were hung on longer pegs.

Color Can Accent

Shaker rooms are pared down to essentials in color as well as shapes, taking their interest from the juxtaposition of the tones of clay pottery, copper kettles, tin utensils, and wood. Yet the Shakers knew the value of using bright color on occasion. Here, a bucket sports bright yellow paint. A dash of color adds spark to a room of subtle tones.

Lilo Raymond

126

Think Simple

When objects are similar in shape and compatible in color, group them together and store them on open shelves to make a striking display.

Work in Daily Objects

Daily chores were performed in a spirit of cooperation. We can imagine how the simple act of churning butter became a shared activity.

127

Paint Brightly

The front door is painted bright orange to contrast with the apple-green trim. Note the humorous touch of the light bulb over the door.

Accent the Details

All of the room's details sport a different color. The molding creates a purple line at the chair rail.

HOWARD KAPLAN

128

COUNTRY COLOR

Sometimes it pays to use colors as bright as the rainbow That's what Tom and Kirsten Beeby did in their weekend home, a converted schoolhouse in Wisconsin. Because the 1890s building, with its lighthearted charm, was itself so playful, the Beebys painted all of the architectural details a different—and shocking—color, adding their own playful touch.

129

CREATIVE COPIES

Furniture influences both the style and the attitude that rooms have. It is a room's basic character. By choosing certain types of furniture rooms become either formal, traditional, or contemporary. The material of the furniture itself introduces warmth and color. If your taste tends to be traditional, you are probably drawn to light pine woods, cherry or the darker oak.

Pick a Ladderback

A classic American ladderback chair was adapted in this modernday reproduction. Notice that the arms, turned legs and top finials are robust in feeling—just like the old ones.

The preference echoed in recent years has been for lighter woods although some antique provincial pieces in the darker woods make great accents. Picture, for instance, a room of stripped pine furniture with one dropleaf table stained black. Painted furniture, the antiques that are so avidly collected today, bring more visual relief in a room of primarily light wood tones.

If you cannot find, or cannot afford, antique furniture do not hesitate to use good reproductions. Look for those that do have the authentic details of the originals. Proportions, curved

Get the Spirit

A tavern table gave its basic shape and form to this contemporary nightstand. The ball-turned legs have the spirit of many farmhouse kitchen tables.

TOM McCAVERA

TOM McCAVERA

Wicker was the rage in grandmother's day. This new chair was derived from a 1930s chair found in an antique shop in North Carolina.

arms, turned legs, finials, should all be closely patterned after the originals. Develop your ability to distinguish these features by visiting museums, historic houses, and fine antique shops.

The chairs that are pictured here, for example, are contemporary copies. But see how the Open Home designers have incorporated those antique details into the modernday design. Best of all, these new chairs can easily be combined with antiques you may own or may still purchase. They share the same spirit. This is another instance of the evolution of America's design.

Use a Copy

The cattail motif of the back splats of this new Windsor dining chair was patterned after a farmhouse chair found in upstate New York.

TOM McCAVERA

TOM McCAVERA

COUNTRY FLAVORS

The color of the foods themselves can be the starting point for your choice of accessories. Take the shiny green of Granny Smith apples and the strong yellow of cheddar cheese; simple as these elements are, they are enough to build color schemes around. That is, in fact, how the most eye-catching table arrangements begin. Whenever you think about the food being served, consider its color and also the colors that complement it. Orange, yellow, green played against the natural wood of a pine table turn this into a delightful setting.

Shape and Pattern

A placemat shaped like a heart adds a playful contrast of shapes at each place setting. The random berry print is edged in color. Notice that some of the plates share the same print and they are mixed with solid color plates and bowls. We repeat —dishes don't have to match!

Napkin Folding

There is more than one way to fold a napkin. Indeed, folding the napkin is limited only by your own imagination. Neither does the napkin have to be placed beside the plate. It's much more fun to fold it into accordian pleats and then place it like a fan inside the soup bowl.

TOM McCAVERA

Shopping for Tablewares

Think creatively when you go out to shop for tablewares. The stores are full of great looking dishes, flatware, and linens. Shown, for instance, are "Berry Patch" dinnerware and placemats from the Open Home collection.

Express Yourself

Indulge your taste in collecting even if it runs to oddities. The ceramic cabbages in the collection delight the eye because they are so funny and fanciful.

Group Them

ndividually, these
ceramics would lack
mpact. En masse,
they form an amus-
ng collection. Notice
hat other vegetables,
such as squash and
eggplant, interject
ouches of color.

COLLECTIBLES

Collecting has become a pastime—and passion—for countless Americans. Almost everyone falls in love with some form of object or oddity. Country things, especially, are in demand, probably because they do fit so beautifully into today's interiors. The objects of our desires—even those that are eccentric—are precisely the things that bring rooms to life.

Collect by Color

The delightful shapes of this ceramic collection are left out on display. The pine cupboard is topped by an amusing cow.

BARRY O'ROURKE/ STOCK MARKET

135

TREE SHUTTERS

When design isn't taken too seriously wonderfully creative rooms result. Chicago architect Tom Beeby and his wife, Kirsten, went looking for a weekend place, and they found a one-room schoolhouse sitting in the cornfields near Beloit, Wisconsin. (It is shown on the last page of this book.) Dating from the 1890s, the schoolhouse had at one time been used

Cut Out a Shutter

The windows were long gone so the couple replaced them. They also added the shutters with cutouts shaped like pine trees.

Shop Around

The Beebys found most of the furniture in local antique and used-furniture shops. Some are fine regional antiques; the rest are "making do." Small benches, for example, function as either seats or pull-up tables, and they sport shocking colors, adding to the house's down-home charm.

as a barn and was in disrepair. Parts of the wainscoted walls had been eaten away by weather, and the roof had a hole in it. The couple bought new wainscoting, which is still sold in some lumberyards, and completely restored the building, converting it for weekend use. Because all of the living takes place in the former schoolroom, the Beebys *couldn't* take design too seriously. They painted the interiors in many colors—apple-green below the chair rail, purple dado trim, and bright orange doors. "We wanted the joy of a summer day inside," the architect said.

Color the Trim

The apple-green of the trim is a color taken from nature, but it shocks in this colorful context.

Lay Down a Rug

An old woven rug, mellowed through years of use, puts a subtle strip on the pine floors.

COPPER STORAGE

TALLIC
CENTS

uster of cop-
pots sends
kling reflec-
s through
country
hen. Don't
erestimate
ower of
allic accents
eative color
mes.

RED BARNS
RED APPLES

Red hearts, checkerboards, red schoolhouses, red brick, and cherry red—red is one of the colors that most characterizes America. Traveling across the country, you'll notice that most barns are red. And in cities, red brick is the standard building material of most turn-of-the-century mills, factories, and warehouses. Many historic houses have a "red room." The one in the White House is an example. Reds are fiery, hot, passionate, and explosive. When you use red in a room it sends off shock-waves. In the rooms and details throughout this section, you'll see how best to use red. Red flowers add flash to a centerpiece; red placemats and napkins grab the attention in a table setting. While reds are best used in small doses, there are also muted reds that are quiet enough to paint on the walls. Certain shades of red are toned down almost to their neutral state. Think of brick red, rust red, the red stain of old painted furniture or of an ancient barn weathered by exposure. Reds mix naturally with anything neutral and, of course, with natural woodgrain. Red is the color used to enrage the bull. In a room, it tends to take over, so use it with a sure hand.

RED

Michael Skott

NATURE'S BOUNTY

Apples, dappled with dew, signify all the variety of luscious reds, greens, and yellows from nature's bounty.

RED SCHOOLHOUSE

Little Red Schoolhouse

Generations of Americans learned the three Rs in little red schoolhouses like this one. These delightful one-room buildings still dot the countryside in rural areas. Located in Sagaponack, Long Island, this schoolhouse has shingle siding, painted red. The white trim makes it all the more vibrant.

TRADITION
The Sagaponack School has been in continuous use since it was built in 1885.

WAGON BED c.1850

David Riley

Knock-down Bed

Rope beds that came apart were transported across this country by settlers on the move.

PIONEER PRACTICALITY

DAVID RILEY

The rope bed that accompanied many pioneers across the country is an example of American ingenuity. It consists simply of four posts, four rails, a headboard and a foot rail. The bed is so cleverly designed that it disassembles and packs into a portable stack for transport. The concept could be adapted by woodworkers into a bed for today's use. Here are the scale drawings that illustrate the bed's simplicity. One might prefer, however, to use standard bed clips rather than the three-inch screws to hold the rails in place.

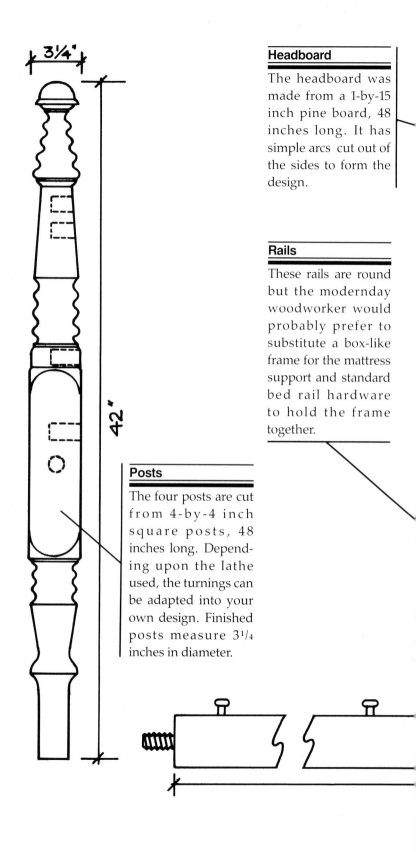

Headboard

The headboard was made from a 1-by-15 inch pine board, 48 inches long. It has simple arcs cut out of the sides to form the design.

Rails

These rails are round but the modernday woodworker would probably prefer to substitute a box-like frame for the mattress support and standard bed rail hardware to hold the frame together.

Posts

The four posts are cut from 4-by-4 inch square posts, 48 inches long. Depending upon the lathe used, the turnings can be adapted into your own design. Finished posts measure 3¹/₄ inches in diameter.

148

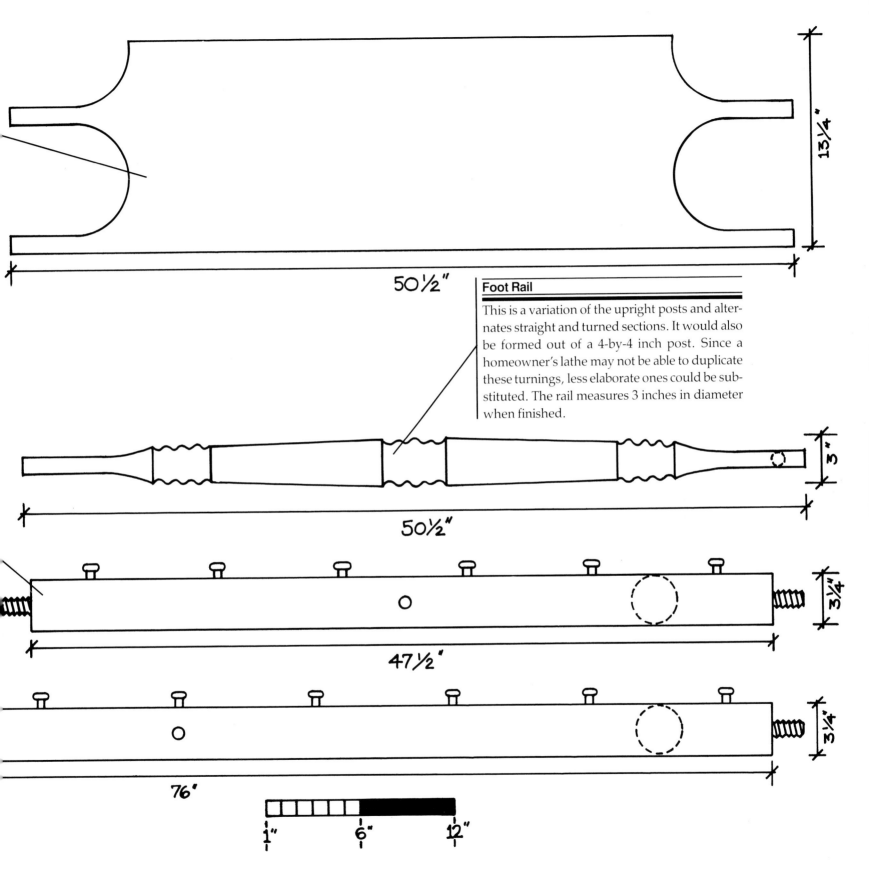

50½"

Foot Rail

This is a variation of the upright posts and alternates straight and turned sections. It would also be formed out of a 4-by-4 inch post. Since a homeowner's lathe may not be able to duplicate these turnings, less elaborate ones could be substituted. The rail measures 3 inches in diameter when finished.

13¼"

3"

50½"

3¼"

47½"

3¼"

76"

1"   6"   12"

Tuck and Fold in New Ways

The wagon bed, top, is waiting for a quick and easy design change. It's accomplished simply by alternating the comforters and folding them in unconventional ways. Take one comforter, for instance, and tuck it in all around the bed; then lay the other, folded flat or rolled up, at the foot of the bed. With a choice of comforters, the bed can take on a variety of transformations whenever you feel the need for a swift style change. If you purchase sheets and comforters that are related in color, you can change the scheme by the day or week.

Give the Bed a Color Change

The marvelous variety of sheets and comforters has opened up a whole new way to dress the bed. Reversible comforters can give the bed two looks, one that's floral and one that's tailored. Coordinating pillow shapes, shams, and bolsters also adds to the stylistic variety. Bed dressing is limited only by imagination. Here's what happens when a large-scale floral comforter pairs with a patchwork-style geometric and with a small dot. Use them together in unexpected treatments, such as these.

Norman McGrath

**STACCATO
RED**
The bold red
the quilt, whi
hangs like a
painting along
the back wall
adds a punch
color to liven
white room's
solid characte

PAINT IT RED

Were you to ask author Marianne Crenshaw what her favorite color is, she would quickly answer: red. Vibrant reds appear throughout her New York City apartment. But it is the way she blends them as staccato counterpoints with her other favorite color, blue, that gives the apartment its visual vitality. In her bedroom, Marianne kept the walls white, as a cool background against which she uses color in bold strokes. The blue-and-white schoolhouse quilt is one strong color statement; the four-poster, painted red, is another.

Hang a Balloon

The author's choice of a bright red balloon poster introduces a round shape as counterpoint to the rectangles of bed and quilt. And it is another bold use of red.

Frances Pelligrini

RAYMOND WAITES

Pin up a Quilt

Early quiltmakers created quilt blocks that have become classic American designs. This fine example deserves to be hung like a painting.

Pick a Red

When you pick a color to use in your home, look at the world outside. The bed is a shade we see in the little red schoolhouse.

Paint it

Marianne purchased her canopy bed from a furniture maker who sells quality reproductions like this one by mail. Instead of leaving it natural, she painted it bright red.

155

RED CHECKERBOARD

Lilo Raymond

Paint a Pattern

The painting, the quilts, and the painted checkerboard pattern around the fireplace are vibrant red, the recurrent theme in this personable country bedroom.

Stencil a quilt

The basic house motif from an old patchwork quilt was interpreted as a stencil pattern on the wall.

BIG RED ROOM

When photographer Hal Davis and his wife converted a schoolhouse in Pine Plains, New York, into a weekend place, they made one of its small rooms into their study. The room may be miniscule but it doesn't lack drama. The Davises accentuated the tight quarters by painting the walls a vivid red and using over-scale furniture that's almost too big for the tiny space. Now that's using color and scale with a sure hand.

Tone it Down

Toning down the vibrant red walls is the Davis's collection of dog paintings.

Accent with Rugs

The many tones of the Oriental rug complement the red walls and bring in other colors.

Think Big

The pine cupboard is really too big for the room; and so is this roll-top desk. But that's what gives the space impact.

MICHAEL SKOTT

158

Look for the Unusual

When you look for antiques, choose those with character, like this unusual barrel chair of mellowed pine. The room's designer was Karin Blake of Los Angeles.

Buy the Best

A fine old comb-back Windsor chair typifies antiques with distinctive personality.

RED AND OLD WOOD

Elyse Lewin

GARDEN MIX

Natural

Blue

Michael Skott

Red

RY
GHTS
primary
s of the
ow are
ed in na-
s harvest—
reds and
, yellow-
pears, and
t oranges.

Orange

Yellow green

GOD BLESS|

Howard Kaplan

Show Your Colors

America is the land of independent spirit. This one-room schoolhouse is dwarfed by the Wisconsin cornfields—but inside it's a cornucopia of color, which you saw on page 128. America's colors, patterns, and forms are free for the taking. Use them. That's what we mean by living home.